Team Spirit

THE ATLANTA HAWKS

BY

MARK STEWART

Content Consultant
Matt Zeysing
Historian and Archivist
The Naismith Memorial Basketball Hall of Fame

NORWOOD HOUSE PRESS

CHICAGO, ILLINOIS

Norwood House Press
P.O. Box 316598
Chicago, Illinois 60631

For information regarding Norwood House Press, please visit our website at:
www.norwoodhousepress.com or call 866-565-2900.

All photos courtesy of Getty Images except the following:
Author's Collection (6, 16, 41 bottom), TCMA, Inc. (7),
Topps, Inc. (9, 30, 34 both, 35 top & bottom right, 36, 40 bottom),
Black Book Partners Archive (14), Dell Publishing Co. (20),
The Star Co. (21, 40 top), Panini USA (22, 39, 41 top),
UPI Telephoto (28), Atlanta Hawks (38, 43), Matthew Richman (48).
Cover Photo: Chris Graythen/Getty Images

Special thanks to Topps, Inc.

Editor: Mike Kennedy
Designer: Ron Jaffe
Project Management: Black Book Partners, LLC.
Research: Joshua Zaffos

Special thanks to Pete Galbiati

Library of Congress Cataloging-in-Publication Data

Stewart, Mark, 1960-
   The Atlanta Hawks / by Mark Stewart ; content consultant, Matt Zeysing.
      p. cm. -- (Team spirit)
   Includes bibliographical references and index.
   Summary: "Presents the history and accomplishments of the Atlanta Hawks
basketball team. Includes highlights of players, coaches, and awards,
quotes, timelines, maps, glossary and websites"--Provided by publisher.
   ISBN-13: 978-1-59953-281-3 (library edition : alk. paper)
   ISBN-10: 1-59953-281-6 (library edition : alk. paper) 1. Atlanta Hawks
(Basketball team)--History--Juvenile literature. I. Zeysing, Matt. II.
Title.
   GV885.52.A7S85 2009
   796.323'6409758231--dc22

                                                      2008039804

COVER PHOTO: The Hawks celebrate a victory during the 2007–08 season.

Table of Contents

SPORTS WORDS & VOCABULARY WORDS: In this book, you will find many words that are new to you. You may also see familiar words used in new ways. The glossary on page 46 gives the meanings of basketball words, as well as "everyday" words that have special basketball meanings. These words appear in **bold type** throughout the book. The glossary on page 47 gives the meanings of vocabulary words that are not related to basketball. They appear in ***bold italic type*** throughout the book.

BASKETBALL SEASONS: Because each basketball season begins late in one year and ends early in the next, seasons are not named after years. Instead, they are written out as two years separated by a dash, for example 1944–45 or 2005–06.

Meet the Hawks

A hawk is a *lethal* hunter. When it strikes, it swoops in with great speed and little sound. The animal it pursues has no chance to escape.

The Atlanta Hawks live up to their name in two ways—they are fast and athletic. They are hardly silent, however. When the Hawks take the court, they bring great excitement and confidence with them. They will trade baskets with any team in the **National Basketball Association (NBA)**.

The players on the Hawks come from many parts of the world and have very different backgrounds. But when they pull on their jerseys, they are all sons of Atlanta, Georgia. Few places welcome players the way the Peachtree City does.

This book tells the story of the Hawks. They play hard and have fun but never lose sight of the prize—a championship banner. They got one in another city more than 50 years ago. The Hawks and their fans have been eager for the next one ever since.

Joe Johnson and Marvin Williams slap a high five during a 2007–08 game.

Way Back When

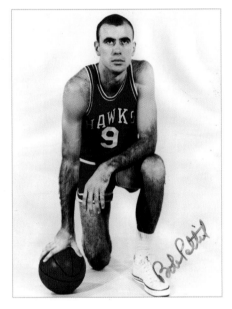

The Hawks played in six different cities before finding a home in Atlanta. The team logged its first 13 games as the Buffalo Bisons. They were new members of the **National Basketball League (NBL)** in 1946–47. The NBL was one of the leagues that later joined together to become the NBA.

After a few weeks, the team decided to move to the Midwest. The Bisons became the Tri-Cities Black Hawks. They made three cities their home: Moline and Rock Island in Illinois and Davenport, Iowa. The star of the Black Hawks was Don Otten. He was one of basketball's first seven-foot centers.

In 1951 the team moved to Milwaukee, Wisconsin and shortened its name to the Hawks. Four years later, the team moved again, this time to St. Louis, Missouri. No matter where they played, the Hawks had trouble winning games. This finally began to change after the team **drafted** a long-armed **power forward** named Bob Pettit in 1954. Later the Hawks traded for Jack Coleman, Jack McMahon, Slater Martin, Ed Macauley, Cliff Hagan, and Alex Hannum. They helped build the core of a championship club.

Hannum became the team's coach and led the Hawks to the **NBA Finals** in 1957. They faced the mighty Boston Celtics and nearly beat them. One year later, the team met Boston again for the league title. This time, the Hawks defeated the Celtics for the NBA Championship. Pettit was the key. He could score from anywhere on the court and was a great rebounder.

The Hawks reached the NBA Finals again in 1960 and 1961, but they lost to the Celtics both times. The team continued to win during the *decade*, as new stars replaced the old. Lenny Wilkens, Richie Guerin, Zelmo Beaty, Bill Bridges, Joe Caldwell, Paul Silas, Walt Hazzard, and Lou Hudson gave the Hawks a powerful **lineup**.

The Hawks loved playing in St. Louis, but the team felt it needed a new arena. The city did not want to build one, so the Hawks began looking for a new home. By the 1968–69 season, they were playing in Atlanta.

The Hawks tried hard to build another champion. Unfortunately, over the next few seasons they lost some good players to the **American Basketball Association (ABA)**. Beaty and Caldwell both ended up in

LEFT: An autographed photo of Bob Pettit.   **ABOVE**: Lenny Wilkens, a great player and later a great coach for the Hawks.

the ABA. Superstar Julius Erving almost became a Hawk but ended up playing in the *rival* league instead. David Thompson and Marvin Webster did the same a few years later.

Even so, the Hawks put some great players on the court. Lou Hudson and Pete Maravich often combined to score more than 50 points a game in the early 1970s. Later in that decade, John Drew, Dan Roundfield, and Tree Rollins teamed up for an awesome front line.

In the 1980s, Dominique Wilkins was the

LOU HUDSON   GUARD-FORWARD

star of the Hawks. He was an unstoppable scorer. His nickname was the "Human Highlight Film" because of his amazing dunks and jump shots. Wilkins once scored 47 points in a **playoff** game against the Celtics. His teammates included Doc Rivers, Kevin Willis, Spud Webb, and Moses Malone.

When Wilkins was traded in the 1990s, the Hawks did not have a superstar to replace him. They continued to win thanks to good players such as Mookie Blaylock, Dikembe Mutombo, and Steve Smith. By the end of the '90s, however, it was time to rebuild the team with younger players.

LEFT: Dominique Wilkins rises for a monster dunk. He was the team's top player during the 1980s.
ABOVE: Lou Hudson, a star for the Hawks in the 1970s.

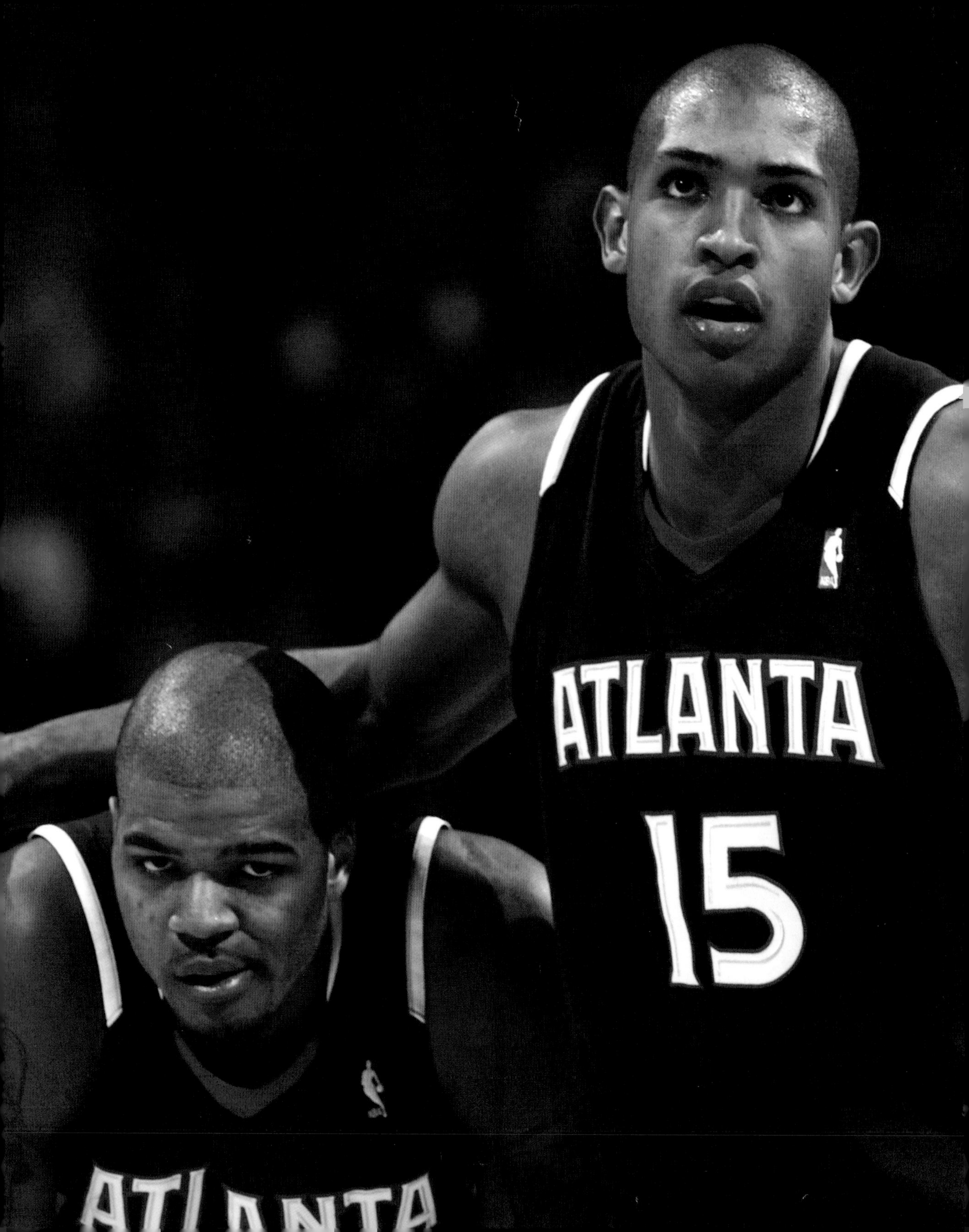
ATLANTA
15
ATLANTA

The Team Today

Through trades and **draft picks**, the Hawks found good building blocks for the future. The team grew up around young players such as Josh Smith, Al Horford, and Acie Law. The Hawks also brought in experienced leaders. Joe Johnson was signed as a **free agent** to a long contract. Mike Bibby also joined the team. In the final seconds of close games, the team looked to these **veterans** to take control.

By the end of the 2007–08 season, the Hawks were playing with new confidence. In the **postseason**, after losing their first two games to the Boston Celtics, the players began to believe in themselves. Led by Johnson and Smith, Atlanta took three of the next four games. The Celtics won Game 7, but they had a new respect for the kids from "A-Town."

Winning respect is important. It is the first step to winning a championship. The Hawks and their fans have been waiting a long time for an NBA title in Atlanta. They believe the team will one day reach that goal.

Josh Smith gets encouragement from Al Horford during a 2007–08 game.

Home Court

When the Hawks played in St. Louis, their home was the Kiel Auditorium. It was named after Henry Kiel. He was the city's mayor from 1913 to 1925.

For most of their history in Atlanta, the Hawks played in the Omni. It was a *futuristic* arena. Some people said it looked like a spaceship. Others said it looked like an upside-down waffle iron. The Omni was part of a group of buildings that included the CNN Center and the Georgia Dome.

In 1999, the Hawks moved into a new arena. It was built on the same site as the Omni. The only reminder of the old building is the scoreboard. It hangs in a *pavilion* in the new arena. The seats in the Hawks' arena are laid out on three sides of the court. The fourth side contains luxury boxes and special "club" seats. The Hawks share the building with the Atlanta Thrashers hockey team.

BY THE NUMBERS

- *There are 18,729 seats for basketball in the Hawks' arena.*
- *The arena cost $213.5 million to build in 1999.*
- *The arena uses "see-through" 24-second shot clocks which don't block views of the court.*

Excited fans in Atlanta cheer the Hawks before a 2007–08 game.

Dressed for Success

During their years in St. Louis, the Hawks used red, white, and blue as their team colors. They kept them for two years after moving to Atlanta. In 1970–71, the Hawks unveiled a modern uniform style with green and blue as the main colors.

They switched back to red as their main color in the mid-1970s. Atlanta used it for more than 30 years—along with other colors such as black and yellow. For the 2007–08 season, the Hawks changed back to blue as their main uniform color.

The Hawks' first *logo* was a bird wearing a basketball uniform. In the 1970s, the team changed to a hawk's head inside a circle. In the 1990s, the Atlanta logo featured a hawk with its wings spread and a basketball clutched in its *talons*. The team still uses this logo.

Walt Bellamy models the team's green and blue uniform from the 1970s.

UNIFORM BASICS

The basketball uniform is very simple. It consists of a roomy top and baggy shorts.

- The top hangs from the shoulders, with big "scoops" for the arms and neck. This style has not changed much over the years.

- Shorts, however, have changed a lot. They used to be very short, so players could move their legs freely. In the last 20 years, shorts have actually gotten longer and much baggier.

Basketball uniforms look the same as they did long ago … until you look very closely. In the old days, the shorts had belts and buckles. The tops were made of a thick cotton called "jersey," which got very heavy when players sweated. Later, uniforms were made of shiny *satin*. They may have looked great, but they did not "breathe." Players got very hot! Today, most uniforms are made of *synthetic* materials that soak up sweat and keep the body cool.

Acie Law drives to the basket in the team's 2007–08 home uniform.

We Won!

For ten seasons in the 1950s and 1960s, the Hawks had one of the best teams in the NBA. From 1957 to 1961, St. Louis reached the league finals four times. Six players made up the heart of the 1956–57 team. Slater Martin and Jack McMahon were the guards, while Jack Coleman, Ed Macauley, and Cliff Hagan lined up as forwards. Bob Pettit played center much of the time.

The Hawks faced the Boston Celtics in the 1957 NBA Finals. Game 7 was one of the best ever. The score was tied after 48 minutes and again after an **overtime** period. The Celtics won 125–123 when a last-second shot by Pettit rolled out of the basket.

One year later the same two teams met again. This time the Hawks were ready for Boston. They beat the Celtics in Game 1 by a score of 104–102. After the Celtics tied the series, the Hawks got the break they needed in Game 3. Bill Russell, the only player on the Celtics who could guard Pettit, hurt his ankle. The Hawks won 111–98.

The Hawks used Russell's injury to their advantage for the rest of the series. Again and again, they drove to the basket for layups. They fought the Celtics hard for every rebound. Boston's super-fast offense got slower and slower.

Still, Boston was a dangerous team. The Celtics won Game 4 in St. Louis to even the series. With the fans in Boston cheering them on, the Celtics nearly won Game 5. The Hawks made the winning plays in the final minutes to escape with a 104–102 victory.

The Hawks looked to Pettit in Game 6. He had been a talented center in college. But when he came to the NBA, he was not sure if he was good enough to succeed against tougher competition. Pettit quickly realized he could make baskets from all over the court. He worked hard to become a great scorer.

LEFT: An autographed photo of Cliff Hagan.
ABOVE: This team photo shows the 1957–58 champs.

Pettit showed just how great he was against Boston. He poured in 31 points in the first three periods of Game 6. The Celtics kept the score close, but they simply could not stop Pettit. He was even better in the fourth quarter. Of the Hawks' final 21 points, Pettit scored 19. The last two came on a tip-in of a missed shot by Martin. With that basket, Pettit reached 50 points, and the Hawks celebrated a 110–109 win—and the NBA Championship.

The Hawks and Celtics had two more championship battles. Boston defeated the Hawks in the 1960 NBA Finals. It was another amazing seven-game battle. In 1961, the Celtics won again, this time in five games.

In 2008—almost 50 years later—the Hawks again met the Celtics in the playoffs. Boston was supposed to destroy the young, inexperienced Hawks. But Atlanta had a surprise. With the home crowd roaring encouragement, the Hawks won every game played in Atlanta. It took the Celtics seven thrilling games to beat the Hawks again.

ABOVE: Bob Pettit battles Bill Russell of the Boston Celtics.
RIGHT: Mike Bibby shoots a jump shot during Atlanta's 2008 playoff matchup with Boston.

Go-To Guys

To be a true star in the NBA, you need more than a great shot. You have to be a "go-to guy"—someone teammates trust to make the winning play when the seconds are ticking away in a big game. Hawks fans have had a lot to cheer about over the years, including these great stars …

THE PIONEERS

BOB PETTIT   6´ 9˝ Forward/Center

• BORN: 12/12/1932   • PLAYED FOR TEAM: 1954–55 TO 1964–65

When it came to putting a basketball through the hoop, few players have ever matched Bob Pettit. He could score in every way imaginable. Pettit was named **Rookie of the Year** in 1954 and was voted the **Most Valuable Player (MVP)** twice.

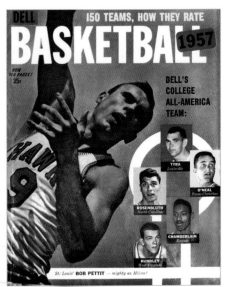

CLIFF HAGAN   6´ 4˝ Forward

• BORN: 12/9/1931

• PLAYED FOR TEAM: 1956–57 TO 1965–66

Cliff Hagan could play any position on the court. Against bigger opponents, he used his unstoppable hook shot. Against smaller opponents, he relied on his powerful body. Hagan averaged over 20 points a game four years in a row.

LENNY WILKENS   6´1˝ Guard

• BORN: 10/28/1937   • PLAYED FOR TEAM: 1960–61 TO 1967–68

Lenny Wilkens was a bright student who was offered less money by the Hawks than he would have made in the business world. Luckily, he chose the NBA. Wilkens was an **All-Star** five times for the Hawks—and later became an excellent coach.

LOU HUDSON   6´5˝ Forward/Guard

• BORN: 7/11/1944   • PLAYED FOR TEAM: 1966–67 TO 1976–77

Lou Hudson combined the dribbling, passing, and shooting skills of a guard with the strength and power of a forward. He scored the first-ever basket for the Hawks after they moved to Atlanta.

PETE MARAVICH   6´5˝ Guard

• BORN: 6/22/1947   • DIED: 1/5/1988

• PLAYED FOR TEAM: 1970–71 TO 1973–74

With his long hair and floppy socks, Pete Maravich did not look like an All-Star. But he played like one. Maravich amazed fans with his *extraordinary* passing and shooting. He teamed with Lou Hudson and Walt Bellamy to give the Hawks three superstars in the early 1970s.

STAR '85

Schick

PETE MARAVICH
Schick NBA Legends Classic

JOHN DREW   6´6˝ Forward

• BORN: 9/30/1954   • PLAYED FOR TEAM: 1974–75 TO 1981–82

John Drew was one of the youngest players in the NBA when he joined the Hawks. In his first season, he led the league in **offensive rebounds**. Drew combined with Dan Roundfield to give Atlanta a great one-two punch.

LEFT: Bob Pettit   **ABOVE**: Pete Maravich

DOMINIQUE WILKINS   6´ 8˝ Forward

- BORN: 1/12/1960 • PLAYED FOR TEAM: 1982–83 TO 1993–94

When Dominique Wilkins jumped, it looked as if he had rockets on his shoes. No one could stop him from dunking, and no one could block his outside shot. Wilkins averaged at least 25 points a game 10 years in a row for the Hawks and won the NBA Slam Dunk Contest twice.

KEVIN WILLIS   7´ 0˝ Center

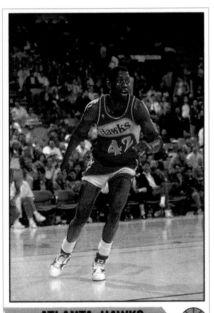

ATLANTA HAWKS
KEVIN WILLIS

- BORN: 9/6/1962
- PLAYED FOR TEAM: 1984–85 TO 1994–95 & 2004–05

Kevin Willis was one of the NBA's best inside players. He was a strong defender and a *ferocious* rebounder. In the 1991–92 season, Willis averaged 18.3 points and 15.5 rebounds per game.

MOOKIE BLAYLOCK   6´ 1˝ Guard

- BORN: 3/20/1967
- PLAYED FOR TEAM: 1992–93 TO 1998–99

Mookie Blaylock was the NBA's biggest "thief" in the 1990s. He stole more passes than anyone on the Hawks—and led the league in steals per game two years in a row. Blaylock was also a good **playmaker** and important team leader. He made the NBA's **All-Defensive Team** six times.

STEVE SMITH   6′ 7″ Guard

- BORN: 3/31/1969
- PLAYED FOR TEAM: 1994–95 TO 1998–99

When the Hawks traded Kevin Willis in 1994, they wanted a player who would be just as talented and popular. Steve Smith filled both roles. He was known for his great shooting and his even greater sportsmanship.

JOSH SMITH   6′ 9″ Forward

- BORN: 12/5/1985
- FIRST SEASON WITH TEAM: 2004–05

Josh Smith went right from high school to the NBA at the age of 19. In his first season, he won the Slam Dunk Contest. Smith soon became one of the best shot-blockers in the NBA.

JOE JOHNSON   6′ 7″ Guard

- BORN: 6/29/1981
- FIRST SEASON WITH TEAM: 2005–06

The Hawks signed Joe Johnson because of his ability to *seize* control of a game. He quickly developed into one of the toughest and most talented scorers in team history. Johnson averaged 20 points a game in his first three seasons in Atlanta.

LEFT: Kevin Willis   **ABOVE**: Steve Smith

On the Sidelines

The Hawks have always been known for getting the most out of the talent on their team. This is where smart coaching comes into play. Since the 1940s, the Hawks have had several excellent coaches. In their early years, Red Auerbach and Red Holzman worked on the sidelines. Auerbach later coached the Boston Celtics to nine championships—including three against the Hawks. Holzman coached the New York Knicks to two NBA titles.

The coach of the Hawks' 1958 championship team was Alex Hannum. He had been a smart player for St. Louis before being named coach. Hannum understood how **role players** could make a team's star better, and how a star could make his teammates better.

Other top coaches for the Hawks included Harry Gallatin, Richie Guerin, Hubie Brown, Mike Fratello, and Lenny Wilkens. In the years since the Hawks moved to Atlanta in 1968, they have had some interesting owners, too. They include Ted Turner and Carl Sanders, the former governor of Georgia. Turner's cable television network, TBS, showed Hawks games to fans all over the country.

Lenny Wilkens discusses a play with his team. He coached the Hawks for seven seasons.

One Great Day

If basketball is a big man's game, then there should be no room in the NBA Slam Dunk Contest for "little men." Someone forgot to tell that to Spud Webb. Although he stood just 5′ 7″, he made a name for himself in **pro** basketball with his many skills, including his incredible leaping ability.

Webb's most *remarkable* moment came during All-Star Weekend in 1986. The year before, teammate Dominique Wilkins had won the Slam Dunk Contest. Wilkins stood 6′ 8″ and could jump as high as anyone in the league. Many thought he would steal the show again in 1986. Webb had a different idea. When he was invited to participate in the contest, he got ready to put on a show of his own.

Webb looked like a child standing next to Wilkins. But then the dunks began. Webb was slamming the ball with ease. The fans roared their delight every time he threw one down. The most surprised person in the arena was Wilkins. He had never seen Webb dunk!

Webb did a one-handed dunk, catching his own pass off the backboard. He did a 360-degree dunk and a backwards double-pump

Spud Webb soars above the rim for the second of his two "perfect" dunks.

dunk. Webb's best jam came after he bounced the ball hard off the floor and high into the air. He took off while the ball was still rising, snatched it with both hands and slammed it through the hoop backwards. The judges gave Webb perfect scores for both of his dunks against Wilkins in the finals. He won the contest easily.

Atlanta coach Mike Fratello knew Webb had planned a big surprise, but he kept the secret from Wilkins. "He told 'Nique he never had anything prepared, didn't practice for it," Fratello remembers. "So 'Nique maybe thought his normal assortment would be good enough to get through."

It wasn't. On this day, Webb proved that big things sometimes come in small packages.

Legend Has It

Which NBA team played its games in an Opera House?

LEGEND HAS IT that the Hawks did. During its days in St. Louis, the team played in Kiel Auditorium. It was a huge building that was also used for operas. A heavy curtain separated the basketball court from the stage. In the summer of 1961, Kiel Auditorium hosted a musical performance about a basketball team. The director knew where to go for actors. When the show opened, several members of the Hawks were part of the cast!

ABOVE: This may look like a basketball game, but it's actually a musical performance featuring members of the Hawks.　**RIGHT**: Ben Kerner

What was the best—and worst—trade the Hawks ever made?

LEGEND HAS IT that it was their 1956 deal with the Boston Celtics. The Hawks had the second pick in the draft that year. Owner Ben Kerner chose Bill Russell and then agreed to trade the star center to the Celtics. In return, the Hawks received Ed Macauley and Cliff Hagan. "That trade made Boston great," Kerner said later, "but it also made us a contender and led to our championship in 1958, when we beat Russell and Boston."

Which NBA mascot was once suspended for a game?

LEGEND HAS IT that Harry the Hawk was. In 1990, the Hawks were playing the Charlotte Hornets in Atlanta. Some Charlotte fans were being especially loud. Harry shook his tailfeathers at them. The fans threw popcorn at him. Soon, a food fight started. Harry ended it by drenching the fans with water. Everyone had a good laugh—except the Hawks. The next day Harry was told he had gone too far. The team suspended the man inside the costume, Wayne Peay, for a game without pay.

It Really Happened

I n the NBA, the rule is six fouls and you're out of the game. But what happens when all but four players foul out of a game? There is a rule for that, too. That is how Cliff Levingston fouled *into* a game!

In 1986, Atlanta and the Utah Jazz played a long, rough game. Because of injuries to two of their stars, the Hawks only had 10 players. Four Hawks fouled out of the game in the fourth quarter.

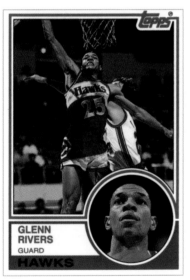

GLENN
RIVERS
GUARD
HAWKS

After 48 minutes, the contest was tied. The game went into overtime. Early in the extra period, Levingston was whistled for his sixth foul and sent to the bench. Only five Hawks were left.

With seven seconds left, guard Doc Rivers got into an argument with a referee. The ref threw Rivers out of the game. Now Atlanta only had four players. Coach Mike Fratello called Levingston's name. The Atlanta forward was shocked. He thought he was done for the night.

Fratello knew that when a team was down to four players, it could send the last player to foul out back into the game. Levingston returned to the action, but he could not save the Hawks. They lost 109–105.

ABOVE: Doc Rivers, whose real name was Glenn.
RIGHT: Cliff Levingston

Team Spirit

Basketball fans in Atlanta have supported the Hawks in good times and bad times. They see the players around town and think of them as neighbors. The team's arena is easy to get to by car or train, so everyone in the Atlanta area can attend the games. Fans are entertained by the A-Town Dancers, the Hawks Spirit Squad, and Harry the Hawk. He is one of the most popular *mascots* in sports. Harry is joined by SkyHawk, who makes acrobatic dunks at halftime.

Atlanta is a popular city for music artists. It is not unusual to see celebrities from the worlds of hip-hop, rock, and country music at Hawks games. Athletes from Atlanta's other teams—including the Falcons, Braves, and Thrashers—are often in the stands. It is an autograph-collector's dream!

When the Hawks came to Atlanta, they left behind thousands of loyal fans in St. Louis. They still miss the team. In 2008, basketball fans there celebrated the 50th anniversary of the Hawks' 1958 championship at the St. Louis Sports Center.

Harry the Hawk loves to entertain the fans during Atlanta home games.

Timeline

The basketball season is played from October through June. That means each season takes place at the end of one year and the beginning of the next. In this timeline, the accomplishments of the Hawks are shown by season.

1946–47
The team plays its first season in four different cities.

1968–69
The Hawks move from St. Louis to Atlanta.

1955–56
Bob Pettit leads the NBA in points and rebounds.

1957–58
The Hawks win the NBA Finals.

1969–70
Bill Bridges and Joe Caldwell make the NBA All-Defensive Team.

Bob Pettit

Bill Bridges

John
Drew

Josh
Smith

1974–75
John Drew leads the NBA
in offensive rebounds.

1999–00
Dikembe Mutombo leads
the NBA in rebounding.

2006–07
Josh Smith becomes
the youngest player to
block 500 shots.

1985–86
Dominique Wilkins
wins the NBA scoring
championship.

1993–94
The Hawks tie a team
record with 57 wins.

2007–08
Joe Johnson scores 20
points in the fourth
quarter of a playoff game.

Mookie Blaylock,
a star on the
1993–94 team.

Joe
Johnson

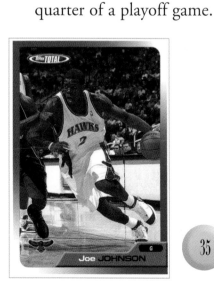

Fun Facts

LET'S BE FRANK

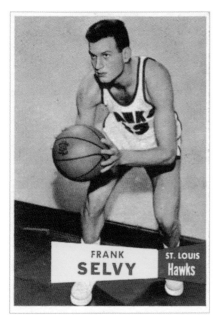

FRANK SELVY

ST. LOUIS Hawks

In 1954, Frank Selvy set an NBA record when he made 24 free throws in a game. Wilt Chamberlain broke his record eight years later— on his way to scoring 100 points in a game!

SHORTENING UP

The Hawks were not named after a bird of prey. They shortened Black Hawks to Hawks in the 1950s. The Black Hawks were named in honor of a Native American chief.

COOL STUFF

Dominique Wilkins specialized in monster dunks. He had two favorites. The first was a windmill dunk, which he often did during games. The second was an off-the-backboard, one-handed tomahawk jam. Wilkins saved this for dunking contests.

ABOVE: Frank Selvy
RIGHT: Tree Rollins swats away a shot attempt.

A TREE GROWS IN GEORGIA

Tree Rollins was a superb shot-blocker. He led the NBA in blocks in 1982–83. Several years earlier, Rollins set a team record when he blocked 12 shots in a game against the Portland Trailblazers.

CHILD'S PLAY

When Josh Smith joined the Hawks, Dominique Wilkins helped him adjust to life in the NBA. When Smith won the 2005 NBA Slam Dunk contest, he wore a Dominique Wilkins jersey as a *Thank You* to his new friend.

BEST BOSS

In 1962–63, the NBA announced that it would begin a new award—**Coach of the Year**. The first winner was Harry Gallatin. He led the Hawks to 48 victories that season.

COUNT IT!

In a 1992 game against the Golden State Warriors, Stacy Augmon scored the six millionth point in NBA history.

Talking Hoops

"Every time a shot goes up, I believe the rebound is mine and I go after it … I know I'm not going to get every one, but the more you try for, the more you get."

—Moses Malone, on how he grabbed so many offensive rebounds

"We're so young and athletic that we can make it tough on a lot of teams."

—Joe Johnson, on the Hawks' team spirit

"I love to get a rise out of the crowd. That's what it's all about."

—Pete Maravich, on his entertaining style of play

ABOVE: Moses Malone   **RIGHT**: Dominique Wilkins

"I play with a great bunch of players. They set me up. They're very, very unselfish. They're the ones who are responsible for my success."

—*Bob Pettit, on the great Hawks teams of the 1950s*

"You've got to have fun. This is what basketball is about."

—*Dominique Wilkins, on why fans loved watching him play*

ATLANTA HAWKS
DOMINIQUE WILKINS

"I don't want to say it's being an ***intimidator****. I just want to help my team control the paint. I don't want anybody coming in thinking that they have an easy layup."

—*Josh Smith, on his shot-blocking style*

"Lou Hudson is basketball's greatest offensive machine."

—*Walt Hazzard, on the amazing ability of his All-Star teammate*

"He could play in any era because he came to play every night. He was a professional on and off the court."

—*Lenny Wilkens, on Bob Pettit*

For the Record

The great Hawks teams and players have left their marks on the record books. These are the "best of the best" …

Bob Pettit

HAWKS AWARD WINNERS

WINNER	AWARD	SEASON
Bob Pettit	Rookie of the Year	1954–55
Bob Pettit	All-Star Game MVP	1955–56
Bob Pettit	Most Valuable Player	1955–56
Bob Pettit	All-Star Game MVP	1957–58
Bob Pettit	All-Star Game co-MVP	1958–59
Bob Pettit	Most Valuable Player	1958–59
Bob Pettit	All-Star Game MVP	1961–62
Harry Gallatin	Coach of the Year	1962–63
Richie Guerin	Coach of the Year	1967–68
Hubie Brown	Coach of the Year	1977–78
Dominique Wilkins	Slam Dunk Champion	1984–85
Spud Webb	Slam Dunk Champion	1985–86
Mike Fratello	Coach of the Year	1985–86
Dominique Wilkins	Slam Dunk Champion	1989–90
Lenny Wilkens	Coach of the Year	1993–94
Dikembe Mutombo	Defensive Player of the Year	1996–97
Alan Henderson	Most Improved Player	1997–98
Dikembe Mutombo	Defensive Player of the Year	1997–98
Josh Smith	Slam Dunk Champion	2004–05

Dominique Wilkins

HAWKS ACHIEVEMENTS

ACHIEVEMENT	SEASON
Western Division Champions	1956–57
Western Division Champions	1957–58
NBA Champions	1957–58
Western Division Champions	1958–59
Western Division Champions	1959–60
Western Division Champions	1960–61
Western Division Champions	1969–70
Central Division Champions	1979–80
Central Division Champions	1986–87
Central Division Champions	1993–94

ATLANTA HAWKS
ANTHONY WEBB

RIGHT: Spud Webb, whose real name was Anthony.
BELOW: The 1959–60 Hawks

ST. LOUIS
HAWKS

Pinpoints

The history of a basketball team is made up of many smaller stories. These stories take place all over the map—not just in the city a team calls "home." Match the push-pins on these maps to the Team Facts and you will begin to see the story of the Hawks unfold!

TEAM FACTS

1   Atlanta, Georgia—*The Hawks have played here since the 1968–69 season.*

2   Baton Rouge, Louisiana—*Bob Pettit was born here.*

3   Little Rock, Arkansas—*Joe Johnson was born here.*

4   St. Louis, Missouri—*The team won the NBA Championship here in 1958.*

5   Highland Park, Michigan—*Steve Smith was born here.*

6   Greensboro, North Carolina—*Lou Hudson was born here.*

7   New Bern, North Carolina—*Walt Bellamy was born here.*

8   Brooklyn, New York—*Lenny Wilkens was born here.*

9   Hobbs, New Mexico—*Bill Bridges was born here.*

10   Los Angeles, California—*Kevin Willis was born here.*

11   Puerto Plata, Dominican Republic—*Al Horford was born here.*

12   Paris, France—*Dominique Wilkins was born here.*

Dominique Wilkins

Play Ball

Basketball is a sport played by two teams of five players. NBA games have four 12-minute quarters—48 minutes in all—and the team that scores the most points when time has run out is the winner. Most baskets count for two points. Players who make shots from beyond the three-point line receive an extra point. Baskets made from the free-throw line count for one point. Free throws are penalty shots awarded to a team, usually after an opponent has committed a foul. A foul is called when one player makes hard contact with another.

Players can move around all they want, but the player with the ball cannot. He must bounce the ball with one hand or the other (but never both) in order to go from one part of the court to another. As long as he keeps "dribbling," he can keep moving.

In the NBA, teams must attempt a shot every 24 seconds, so there is little time to waste. The job of the defense is to make it as difficult as possible to take a good shot—and to grab the ball if the other team shoots and misses.

This may sound simple, but anyone who has played the game knows that basketball can be very complicated. Every player on the court has a job to do. Different players have different strengths and weaknesses. The coach must mix these players in just the right way, and teach them to work together as one.

The more you play and watch basketball, the more "little things" you are likely to notice. The next time you are at a game, look for these plays:

PLAY LIST

ALLEY-OOP—A play where the passer throws the ball just to the side of the rim—so a teammate can catch it and dunk in one motion.

BACK-DOOR PLAY—A play where the passer waits for his teammate to fake the defender away from the basket—then throws him the ball when he cuts back toward the basket.

KICK-OUT—A play where the ball-handler waits for the defense to surround him—then quickly passes to a teammate who is open for an outside shot. The ball is not really kicked in this play; the term comes from the action of pinball machines.

NO-LOOK PASS—A play where the passer fools a defender (with his eyes) into covering one teammate—then suddenly passes to another without looking.

PICK-AND-ROLL—A play where one teammate blocks or "picks off" another's defender with his body—then cuts to the basket for a pass in the confusion.

Glossary

BASKETBALL WORDS TO KNOW

ALL-DEFENSIVE TEAM—An honor given at the end of each season to the NBA's best defensive players at each position.

ALL-STAR—A player selected to play in the annual All-Star Game.

AMERICAN BASKETBALL ASSOCIATION (ABA)—The basketball league that played for nine seasons starting in 1967. Prior to the 1976–77 season, four ABA teams joined the NBA, and the rest went out of business.

COACH OF THE YEAR—An award given each season to the league's best coach.

DRAFT PICKS—College players selected or "drafted" by NBA teams each summer.

DRAFTED—Chosen from a group of the best college players. The NBA draft is held each summer.

FREE AGENT—A player who is allowed to join any team he wants.

LINEUP—The list of players who are playing in a game.

MOST VALUABLE PLAYER (MVP)—The award given each year to the league's best player; also given to the best player in the league finals and All-Star Game.

NATIONAL BASKETBALL ASSOCIATION (NBA)—The professional league that has been operating since 1946–47.

NATIONAL BASKETBALL LEAGUE (NBL)—An early professional league that played 12 seasons, from 1937–38 to 1948–49, then merged with the Basketball Association of America to become the NBA.

NBA FINALS—The playoff series that decides the champion of the league.

OFFENSIVE REBOUNDS—Rebounds of shots missed by teammates.

OVERTIME—The extra period played when a game is tied after 48 minutes.

PLAYMAKER—Someone who helps his teammates score by passing the ball.

PLAYOFF—Describing the games played after the season to determine the league champion.

POSTSEASON—Another term for playoffs.

POWER FORWARD—The bigger and stronger of a team's two forwards.

PRO—A player or team that plays a sport for money. College players are not paid, so they are considered "amateurs."

ROLE PLAYERS—People who are asked to do specific things when they are in a game.

ROOKIE OF THE YEAR—The annual award given to the league's best first-year player.

VETERANS—Players with great experience.

OTHER WORDS TO KNOW

DECADE—A period of 10 years; also specific periods, such as the 1950s.

EXTRAORDINARY—Unusual, or unusually talented.

FEROCIOUS—Extremely intense.

FUTURISTIC—Very modern.

INTIMIDATOR—Someone who scares or frightens people.

LETHAL—Damaging or destructive.

LOGO—A symbol or design that represents a company or team.

MASCOTS—Animals or people believed to bring a group good luck.

PAVILION—A part of a building that stands out from the rest of the structure.

REMARKABLE—Unusual or exceptional.

RIVAL—Extremely emotional competitor.

SATIN—A smooth, shiny fabric.

SEIZE—To capture or gain.

SYNTHETIC—Made in a laboratory, not in nature.

TALONS—The claws of a bird or animal.

Places to Go

ON THE ROAD

ATLANTA HAWKS
1 Philips Drive
Atlanta, Georgia 30303
(404) 878-3800

NAISMITH MEMORIAL BASKETBALL HALL OF FAME
1000 West Columbus Avenue
Springfield, Massachusetts 01105
(877) 4HOOPLA

ON THE WEB

THE NATIONAL BASKETBALL ASSOCIATION   www.nba.com
 • *Learn more about the league's teams, players, and history*

THE ATLANTA HAWKS   www.nba.com/hawks
 • *Learn more about the Hawks*

THE BASKETBALL HALL OF FAME   www.hoophall.com
 • *Learn more about history's greatest players*

ON THE BOOKSHELF

To learn more about the sport of basketball, look for these books at your library or bookstore:

 • Hareas, John. *Basketball*. New York, New York: DK, 2005.

 • Hughes, Morgan. *Basketball*. Vero Beach, Florida: Rourke Publishing, 2005.

 • Thomas, Keltie. *How Basketball Works*. Berkeley, California: Maple Tree Press, distributed through Publishers Group West, 2005.

Index

The Team

MARK STEWART has written more than 20 books on basketball, and over 100 sports books for kids. He grew up in New York City during the 1960s rooting for the Knicks and Nets, and now takes his two daughters, Mariah and Rachel, to watch them play. Mark comes from a family of writers. His grandfather was Sunday Editor of *The New York Times* and his mother was Articles Editor of *The Ladies Home Journal* and *McCall's*. Mark has profiled hundreds of athletes over the last 20 years. He has also written several books about his native New York, and New Jersey, his home today. Mark is a graduate of Duke University, with a degree in history. He lives with his daughters and wife, Sarah, overlooking Sandy Hook, New Jersey.

MATT ZEYSING is the resident historian at the Basketball Hall of Fame in Springfield, Massachusetts. His research interests include the origins of the game of basketball, the development of professional basketball in the first half of the twentieth century, and the culture and meaning of basketball in American society.